D1432704

First
Facts™

Holidays and Culture

St. Patrick's Day

Day of Irish Pride

by **June Preszler**

Consultant:
David G. Hunter
Professor of Religious Studies, Iowa State University
Ames, Iowa

INDIANAPOLIS MARION CO
PUBLIC LIBRARY

Capstone
press®
Mankato, Minnesota

First Facts is published by Capstone Press,
151 Good Counsel Drive, P.O. Box 669, Mankato, Minnesota 56002.
www.capstonepress.com

Copyright © 2007 by Capstone Press. All rights reserved.
No part of this publication may be reproduced in whole or in part, or stored in a
retrieval system, or transmitted in any form or by any means, electronic, mechanical,
photocopying, recording, or otherwise, without written permission of the publisher.
For information regarding permission, write to Capstone Press,
151 Good Counsel Drive, P.O. Box 669, Dept. R, Mankato, Minnesota 56002.
Printed in the United States of America

Library of Congress Cataloging-in-Publication Data
Preszler, June, 1954–
    St. Patrick's Day : day of Irish pride / by June Preszler.
    p. cm.—(First facts. Holidays and culture)
    Summary: "Describes the history and meaning of St. Patrick's Day and how it is celebrated
today"—Provided by publisher.
    Includes bibliographical references and index.
    ISBN-13: 978-0-7368-6398-8 (hardcover)
    ISBN-10: 0-7368-6398-2 (hardcover)
    1. Saint Patrick's Day—Juvenile literature. I. Title. II. Series.
GT4995.P3P74 2007
394.262—dc22   2006002950

Editorial Credits
Shari Joffe, editor; Biner Design, designer; Juliette Peters, set designer; Jo Miller, photo researcher;
    Scott Thoms, photo editor

Photo Credits
Capstone Press/Karon Dubke, 21
Corbis/Museum of the City of New York, 10; Swim Ink 2, LLC, 16
Getty Images Inc./Archive Photos, 7; Bill Greenblatt, 14; Paul McErlane, 4–5; Showbiz Ireland, 9;
    Tim Boyle, 20; Yoshikazu Tsuno, cover
PhotoEdit Inc./Robin Nelson, 12; Rudi Von Briel, 19
Shutterstock/Jun Xiao, 1, 18; Yare Marketing, 15
Superstock, 8
UNICORN Stock Photos/Robin Rudd, 13

1 2 3 4 5 6 11 10 09 08 07 06

Table of Contents

Celebrating St. Patrick's Day

Green is everywhere. Partygoers wear green hats and decorate their faces. People everywhere are dressed in bright-green clothing. It's St. Patrick's Day, a day of celebrating Irish **culture**.

Fact!

Green is the national color of Ireland. But wearing a lot of green on St. Patrick's Day is an American custom. In Ireland, wearing too much green is considered bad luck.

5

What Is St. Patrick's Day?

St. Patrick's Day began as a way to honor St. Patrick, the **patron saint** of Ireland. Patrick brought **Christianity** from England to Ireland in the 400s. He was named a saint after he died on March 17, 461. Ever since, St. Patrick's Day has been a religious holiday and Irish cultural celebration.

Fact!

A legend says that St. Patrick drove all the snakes out of Ireland. In truth, there have never been snakes in Ireland.

Celebrating in Ireland

Traditionally, people in Ireland celebrated St. Patrick's Day as a holy day. Families went to church in the morning. They feasted and danced in the afternoon.

Today, it is still a holy day, but it is also a festive day of Irish pride. Dublin holds a five-day St. Patrick's Festival that includes parades, music, and fireworks.

10

St. Patrick's Day Comes to America

Irish **immigrants** brought St. Patrick's Day to America. They began to arrive in the 1700s. The Irish did not forget their roots when they came to America. In 1737, Boston became the first American city where St. Patrick's Day was celebrated.

Fact!

The world's first St. Patrick's Day parade was held in New York City in 1762. A group of Irish soldiers serving with the British army held the parade as a show of Irish pride.

Today in the United States

In the United States, people enjoy all things Irish on St. Patrick's Day. They wear green, listen to Irish folk music, and eat Irish food.

Corned beef and cabbage is a favorite St. Patrick's Day meal. Cabbage is a traditional Irish food. Corned beef is a food people think is Irish, but it's not!

13

Shamrocks

On St. Patrick's Day, people around the world wear **shamrocks**. These three-leaf clovers grow wild in Ireland. They are a **symbol** of good luck.

St. Patrick used the shamrock to help
teach people about the Christian faith.
The three shamrock leaves stand for
God, Jesus, and the Holy Spirit.

Leprechauns

Leprechauns are another symbol of St. Patrick's Day. Irish **legend** has it that these tiny elves make the shoes for Ireland's fairies. They are paid in gold, which they hide in a pot at the end of a rainbow. It's said that if you catch a leprechaun, he'll take you to his pot of gold.

A Day of Parades

Many cities around the world hold parades on St. Patrick's Day. Bright, colorful floats roll down streets. Marching bands play Irish music.

The world's largest St. Patrick's Day parade is in New York City. More than 150,000 people march proudly to show their love of Irish culture.

Amazing Holiday Story!

Chicago has a special way of celebrating St. Patrick's Day. Every year, the city dyes the Chicago River a bright shade of Irish green.

The tradition started in 1962. That year, 100 pounds (45 kilograms) of vegetable dye were poured into the river. The water stayed green for a week! Today, only 40 pounds (18 kilograms) of dye are used. It's enough to turn the river green for several hours.

Hands On: Leprechaun Trap

Why catch a leprechaun? Well, a legend says that if you catch one of these playful, tricky little elves, he'll have to take you to his pot of gold at the end of the rainbow!

What You Need

shoebox
aluminum foil
tape or glue
stickers
stick about twice the depth
   of the box

What You Do

1. Remove the shoebox lid.
2. Use aluminum foil to cover the outside of the shoebox. Tape or glue the foil to the box.
3. Decorate the shoebox with stickers.
4. On the night before St. Patrick's Day, set up the leprechaun trap. Stand the stick up with one end touching the floor. Turn the shoebox upside down and rest it on the stick. If a leprechaun passes by and bumps the stick, the box will fall down upon him.

Glossary

Christianity (KRISS-chee-AN-uh-tee)—the religion based on the life and teachings of Jesus

culture (KUHL-chur)—a people's way of life, ideas, art, customs, and traditions

immigrant (IM-uh-gruhnt)—someone who comes from abroad to live permanently in another country

legend (LEJ-uhnd)—a story handed down from earlier times

patron saint (PAY-truhn SAYNT)—a saint who is believed to look after a particular country or group of people; a saint is a person honored by the Catholic church because of his or her very holy life.

shamrock (SHAM-rok)—a small plant with three leaves that is the national symbol of Ireland

symbol (SIM-buhl)—a design or an object that stands for something else

Read More

Bredeson, Carmen. *St. Patrick's Day*. Rookie Read-About Holidays. New York: Children's Press, 2003.

Gillis, Jennifer Blizin. *St. Patrick's Day*. Holiday Histories. Chicago: Heinemann Library, 2003.

Internet Sites

FactHound offers a safe, fun way to find Internet sites related to this book. All of the sites on FactHound have been researched by our staff.

Here's how:

1. Visit *www.facthound.com*

2. Choose your grade level.

3. Type in this book ID **0736863982** for age-appropriate sites. You may also browse subjects by clicking on letters, or by clicking on pictures and words.

4. Click on the **Fetch It** button.

FactHound will fetch the best sites for you!

Index